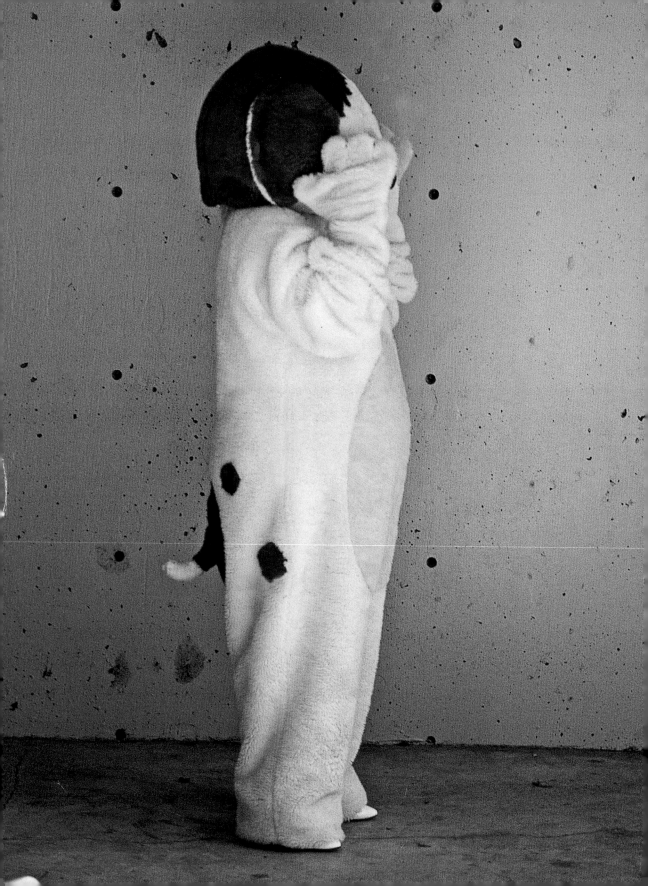

QUINCY THE HOBBY PHOTOGRAPHER

the complete guide
to do→it→yourself
dog photography

J. OTTO SEIBOLD

HARCOURT, INC.

ORLANDO · AUSTIN · NEW YORK · SAN DIEGO · TORONTO · LONDON

Printed in Singapore

TABLE OF CONTENTS

QUINCY THE HOBBY

PHOTOG-RAPHER

HELPFUL HINTS THROUGHOUT THIS BOOK:

Quincy
HELPFUL
PHOTO HINT

CHAPTER I Meet the Author

QUINCY

RENOWNED
HOBBY
PHOTOGRAPHER

HELLO. MY NAME IS

Quincy

WELCOME TO THE FASCINATING WORLD OF DOG PHOTOGRAPHY.

I am prepared to help YOU master the art of hobby photography.

PARDON ME... *click!*

RULE #*1:* *Always be prepared.*

Please read on—

WHAT IS HOBBY
PHOTOGRAPHY?

An excellent question with a fascinating answer!
First things first. Allow me to present you with my
definition of a hobby:
A hobby is anything you like to do that is just for you.

Most people, like me, have jobs. For example, I order
birdseed for a reputable bird-chasing company. This
affords me the nickels and dimes I need to further my
nickel and dime collection (another one of my hobbies).
However, when I'm not on the clock, I can usually be found
concentrating on my primary hobby, dog photography.
You may already have a hobby or two yourself. A hobby
can be anything that you like to do in your free time, be it
riding a bike or collecting records.

I have heard of some unfortunate instances where a person
was fired for spending too much time on his or her hobby.
If this happens to you, don't worry! You can make your
hobby your job! In fact, I know of a popular singing star
who began his career in just this fashion.

So you see, there are very few drawbacks to pursuing your
hobby. My favorite hobby is photographing dogs, and if
you are interested in my art, just follow along with my
handy, helpful guide.

Oops, my break is almost over!

Okay. *Quincy*
H.P.

The ART of dog photography has existed since the invention of the camera. Before that, faithful dogs would sit for hours to have their portraits painted. Photography has made the act of capturing these images much easier on these sometimes restless creatures.

Also, although a painter can change or interpret the essence of a dog in his or her work, a photograph never lies. Therefore, when it comes to matters of accuracy, I believe in the photograph. For now.

In this portion of the book, I have included one of the very oldest examples of dog portraiture from my collection. As you can see, the photograph was taken in black-and-white, or two-tone, film, which is a clear indication that it is very old. You may also see, upon further examination, that the dog is pulling a cart of potatoes, which I believe were a staple of a dog's diet until the early twentieth century.

If this is your first experience with dog photography, rest assured that your new hobby is a noble and time-honored one.

OLD-TIME HOBBYIST
Historic photographer to the kennels
of the Court of Spain. 1869

CHAPTER III

WARDROBE

Some hobbies have certain wardrobe needs, such as snorkeling, beekeeping, and performing martial arts. That is why. . .

I HAD A SPECIAL OUTFIT TAILORED TO MY EXACT FIELD NEEDS.

it's in the "JUMP-SUIT" style.

When I change into my **special** hobby photographer outfit, I am ready to concentrate on one thing: my hobby!

When I'm in my hobby suit, I am ready for action. A suit is not necessary for everyone, but for me it fits.

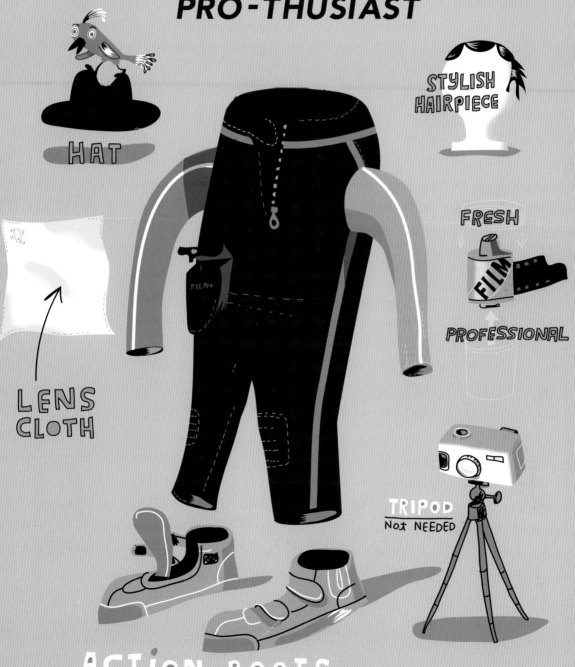

Tools of the MODERN PRO-THUSIAST

HAT

STYLISH HAIRPIECE

LENS CLOTH

FRESH FILM PROFESSIONAL

TRIPOD
Not NEEDED

ACTION BOOTS

CHAPTER IV

HOW A CAMERA WORKS

INSTRUCTIONS

1. LOCATE AUTOMATIC SETTING
2. SET ON AUTOMATIC
3. OKAY, YOU'RE GOOD TO GO

It is that simple.

furthermore

HONORED GUEST Q.H.P.

FLASH guide

Day	Night
Not Recommended	Recommended

I practice at home on my PUBLIC SPEAKING skills. Just in case I am ever invited to lecture at a hobbyist conference.

The figures below demonstrate my personal approach to dog photography.

FIGURE #1

click.

TAKE IT!
TAKE IT!

FIGURE #2

I like to have my film developed in about an hour. So I go to the one-hour photo lab and ask:

"In your estimation, how long will it be until I can see these pictures?"

"About an hour," is the reply.

After that I say nothing.

FIGURE #3

SEE FIGURE #1

SEE FIGURE #2

SEE FIGURE #3

QUINCY'S
How to Take Pictures
(timeline)

CHOOSE FILM

↓

LOAD CAMERA

↓

FIND SUBJECT

↓

take **CLICK** picture

Repeat until out of film.

End of film roll

↓

TAKE FILM TO DEVELOPMENT PROFESSIONALS
CHEMICALS

↓

PICK UP FILM

↓

VIEW PICTURE

KEEP THIS CHART
IN YOUR HEAD

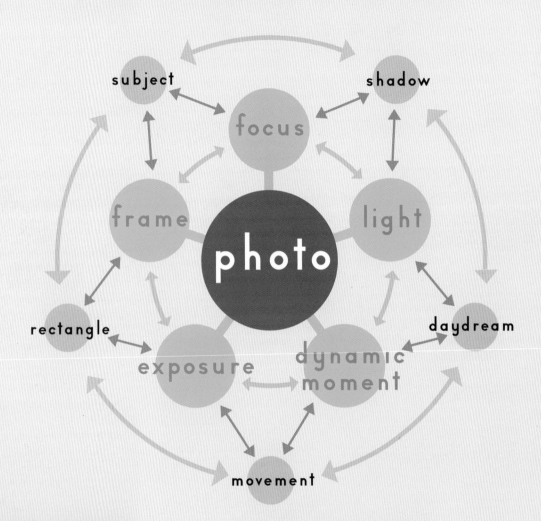

subject

shadow

focus

frame

light

photo

rectangle

daydream

exposure

dynamic moment

movement

QUINCY CHART #1

Study the chart and keep it in mind when conducting your fieldwork.

I have developed this helpful chart to help others.

It represents all of the factors that go through my mind at the exact moment I "release the shutter," which is a fancy way of saying "take the picture."

The blue dots in the outer ring range from creative moods to split decisions.

And the big red dot is the reason you are concentrating on all of the other dots.

The orange dots are more technical in nature.

CHAPTER V

Common (Avoidable) Hazards of Dog Photography

Not every click of the shutter becomes a prizewinning effort. Here are some examples from my library, annotated to help YOU avoid similar hazards.

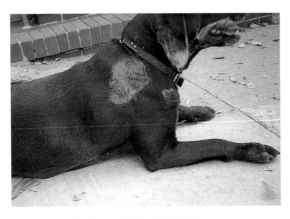

SUBJECT SEEMS "CHALKY"

SUBJECT OUT OF FOCUS
(with exception of nose)

THOUGHTS ABOUT PHOTOGRAPHING DOGS

"Some dogs take no notice of the camera, but others are interested in the strange object and must be allowed to sniff over the equipment and satisfy their curiosity."

– PHILIP JOHNSON
*Focal Encyclopedia of Photography
Desk Edition*

ONE METHOD FOR APPROACHING A dog YOU WISH to PHOTOGRAPH:

1 introduce yourself

HEY THERE

THINGS TO CONSIDER in the PURSUIT of ERROR-FREE PHOTOGRAPHY

But don't be too cautious. Sometimes photos can become what are known as **HAPPY ACCIDENTS**, mistakes that are even better than what you had initially planned.

DOG INATTENTIVE

DOG NOT A DOG

2 Allow subject to sniff camera

3 WHEN SUBJECT APPEARS RELAXED:

CLICK FREELY!

Quincy HELPFUL PHOTO HINT

TOP COMMON AVOIDABLE HAZARDS:
* lens cap left on
* no film / roll full
* batteries dead

The BEST SURPRISE is the PHOTOGRAPH that TURNS OUT BETTER than EVER IMAGINABLE.

DISTRACTIONS

When one is out in the field,
it is important to be alert!
Photographic opportunities
do not often
announce themselves.
My special outfit helps,
of course, but I still can
fall under the spell of
DISTRACTIONS.
Keeping your focus
(and I don't mean your
camera's) allows you to react
to the
DYNAMIC MOMENT
(see chart on page 18)
when it occurs.

Quincy
HELPFUL
PHOTO HINT

You can stop and smell
the roses,
but dogs don't hold their poses.

Sniff

CHAPTER VI Composition
CAPTURING THE RECTANGLE

TALL

WIDE

Life is not a rectangle; a photograph often is.
—QUINCY H.P.

As you've probably noticed when looking at your own pictures, a photograph is, first and foremost, a rectangle!

As a hobby photographer, I accept the privilege and the responsibility of what I call capturing the rectangle.

I fill my rectangle to the best of my ability. I can make it tall or wide. I can fill the box all the way up by moving very close to my subject, or leave a big open space, with a dog off in the distance. These handy tricks change everything about my pictures.

I can make a little dog look like a giant, or make a big dog look like a dot. And then—*CLICK!*—what is in is in, and what is not is gone forever.

Quincy HELPFUL PHOTO HINT

The farther away you are from your subject, the tinier the subject will appear in your photo.

A very good place to fill your rectangle with dogs is at the park....

dogs TALKING on TELEVISION

In my experience I've found that one of the best places to practice my hobby is in the comfort of my own living room. While watching television on rainy afternoons, and sometimes late at night, I have come across increasing numbers of dogs talking in sitcoms, movies, and advertisements. I never miss the opportunity to snap a picture of this phenomenon. If captured correctly, these shots turn out looking like I photographed the dog in person. It's not cheating, it's my hobby!

While practicing this technique, I stumbled upon what is perhaps my best theory: I believe that in the not too distant future, dogs everywhere will begin to talk as a result of seeing their fellow canines speaking in the media.

My hypothesis is based in part on my observation of my own dogs. I already know they understand certain words, like *ball, park,* and *treat.* They also show signs of extreme interest when a talking dog appears on television. I believe this is because they know their own progress is not far off. In addition to this evidence, I have documented many occasions when owners have asked their dogs to speak, and because dogs generally want to please their caregivers, I imagine it is only a matter of time until they fulfill this request.

Until then, I will continue to read out loud to my own dogs, so that when the time comes they will have extensive vocabularies with which they may fully express themselves.

Signed,

Quincy
h.p.

Okay, turn off the lights.

SHAPED, CAGED, and STUFFED

In keeping my photography subject to dogs, I am always on the lookout for them.

This has led me to find that dogs are often in unusual situations. For instance, the dog to the far right is stuffed—it is no longer alive! It is a somewhat famous dog because it had belonged to a famous artist who bought it already stuffed.

After the artist finished living his life, the dog went to a museum, where, to my knowledge, it still stands today!

The dog with the spoon near his mouth was a resident of a small coastal community that is known for removing all road signs that show where it is. The dog didn't belong to anyone and was sort of the unofficial mayor…and he really liked yogurt.

The dog below the mayor was at a folk-art home in Houston, Texas. The house had so many objects stuck all over it that it took me a long time to notice one of them was a dog sticking his head through a hole!

This photograph was taken using the **not looking** technique, which means that I took the photo with the camera behind my back. It wasn't until I had the film developed that I found out about this dog's interest in recycling!

Dogs everywhere love to be in pairs, even in Paris!
Some live together, and some are merely park pals.
Some look alike, and some don't.

Regardless, dogs in pairs know there is always someone
around who likes to do the things they like to do.

DOGS in PAIRS

No need to panic!
The dog in the photo on
the left was merely dressed
up for Halloween. I usually
don't take photos of dogs
in outfits (little Styrofoam
hats are rarely charming),
but this bandaged dog
was so frightfully attired,
I couldn't resist.

The dogs below are both
wild and taxidermied.

The dog on the right
was baking in front of a
chile store.

DOGS in NATURE

Dogs love nature—it's where they are from! They can swim, run around in shrubs, or see other animals.

By the way, I achieved the reflection effect on the opposite page by mirroring the image— a little *darkroom magic!*

DOGS in STORES

More and more, I see dogs in stores.
Early in my career, I found most dogs tied up
outside of stores, so I did not need to go into
stores myself. But when I finally went into one,
I found out that not only were dogs outside
of stores, there were dogs IN stores! And
especially pet stores! But beware, photos taken
in pet stores (as shown on the right) can be
quite emotionally powerful.

Dogs in stores are not always merely shopping.
The dog on the left worked at an outdoor food
stand performing a variety of tasks, none of
which I saw because he was, as I imagined, on
a well-deserved break.

Some dogs are MADE IN CHINA.

DOGS in CARS

Aside from humans, no other animals I know are as at ease in a motor vehicle as dogs.

Have you ever seen a parakeet parked patiently in a lot, waiting for its owner?

Photographing dogs in cars is very easy and has afforded me many interesting pictures. I encourage you to try it yourself.

51

A further note about photographing dogs in cars: Automobile windows create a natural frame-within-a-frame effect.

Fine photographs are often framed and placed under glass. When dogs are photographed in cars, you get both—a frame *and* glass— without a trip to the frame shop!

TOUGH CHOICES

One of the hardest parts of this hobby is choosing the better of two of your own photos. That is why I usually stick to my "one photo per dog" rule. This way I never have to choose which picture is the best. However, sometimes I break my own rule and end up with two very similar images. When faced with this dilemma, I often choose *not* to choose and instead include both pictures, as I have done with the photos below.

Now that you are well on your way to becoming an expert hobby photographer, you will find that you will have to decide which of your photos to share, and which to omit. Doing so is an important part of the process. This is called **editing**, and it's tough.

OLD DOGS

I like to photograph old dogs because they always look me in the eye as if I were an old friend. And because they are old, I trust that they are right. Some old dogs can be very sweet and shy. Others can be set in their ways and a little bit cranky. No matter their mood, I always show old dogs the same respect and consideration I give to all of my canine subjects.

I also am always sure to thank them for their time and give them a friendly scratch if possible.

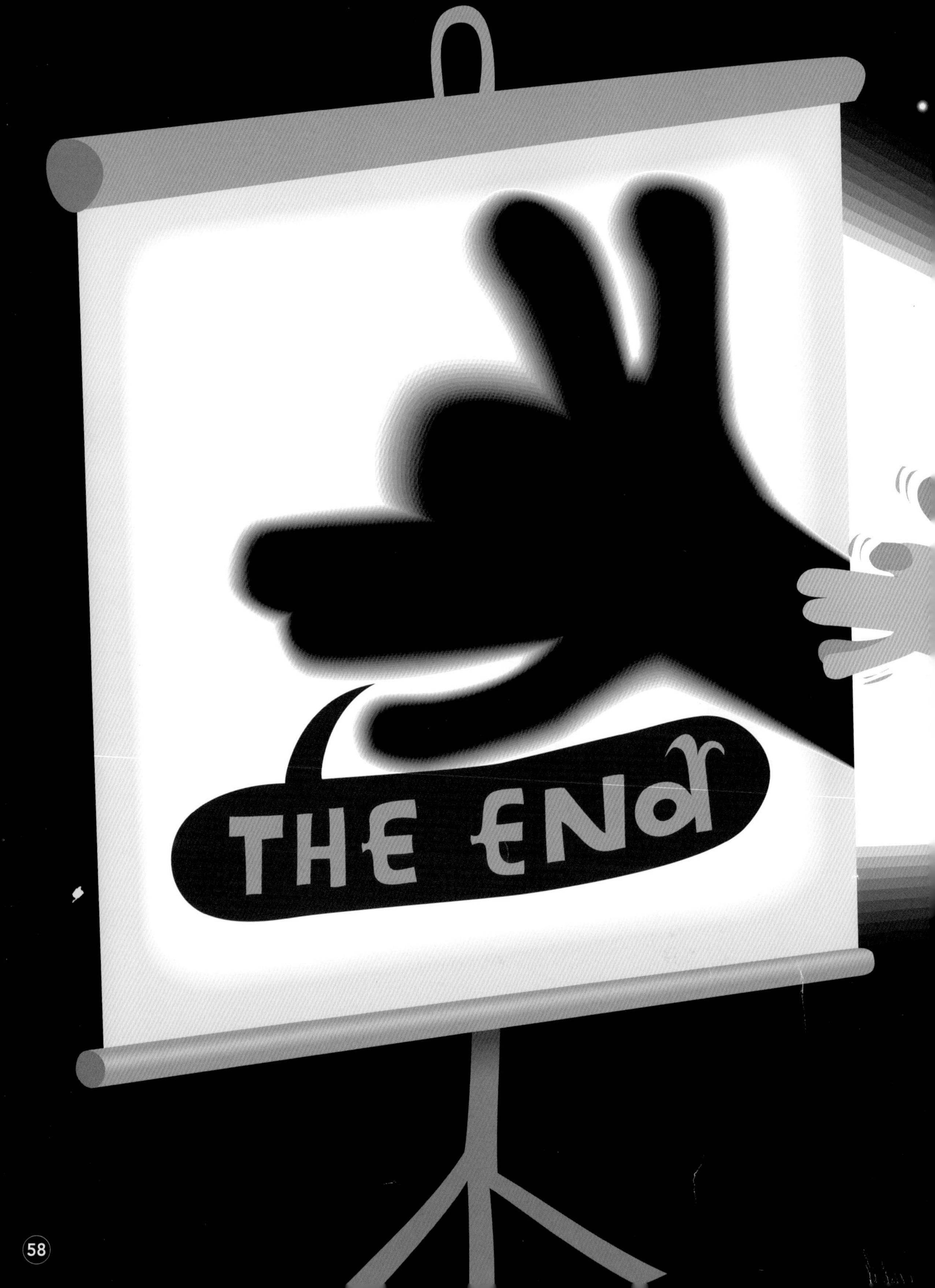
THE END

Okay, that's it: time for bed....
A good night's sleep is the hobbyist's
best preparation!

59

You have reached the end of my informative and insightful book.

The knowledge contained within is now yours to use. Freely!

Quincy
HELPFUL PHOTO HINT

Everyone and everything in life can be beautiful.
It is just a matter of how you frame it.
And it is not necessary to limit your subject to dogs.

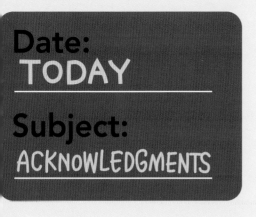

Date:
TODAY

Subject:
ACKNOWLEDGMENTS

in memory of the champ and the BABY 1990 — 2005

The essays in this book were greatly shaped by the fanciful writing of Darcie Edgemon, the love of my life.

Photograph page 33: Cecil from The Andy Warhol Museum archives, 1960s; Founding Collection, The Andy Warhol Museum, Pittsburgh; used with permission.
Photograph page 40 (bottom): from the American Museum of Natural History, Special Collections, New York; used with permission.

www.HarcourtBooks.com

Library of Congress Cataloging-in-Publication Data
Seibold, J.otto.
Quincy, the hobby photographer:
volume one, dogs/J.otto Seibold.—1st ed.
p. cm.
Summary: Quincy, snappy dresser and world-renowned photographer, gives an introduction to his favorite hobby, taking pictures of dogs.
[1. Photography—Fiction. 2. Dogs—Fiction. 3. Humorous stories.]
I. Title.
PZ7.S45513Qui 2006
[Fic]—dc22   2005009422
ISBN-13: 978-0-15-101494-1   ISBN-10: 0-15-101494-9

First edition

H G F E D C B A

The display and text types were set in fonts
including Avenir, Honky, and Bulmer.
Color separations by Colourscan Co. Pte. Ltd., Singapore
Printed and bound by Tien Wah Press, Singapore
This book was printed on totally chlorine-free Stora Enso Matte paper.
Production supervision by Jane Van Gelder
Designed by Lauren Rille

Much appreciation to **Michael Stearns** for his endless patience and cantankerous wit, and to **Samantha McFerrin** for her positive perseverance, and to everyone at Harcourt for their encouragement and support.

And special thanks to Matt Eller at **FEELGOODANYWAY** for his graphic graciousness.

The illustrations in this book were done on a Macintosh computer using Adobe Illustrator software and drawn on a Wacom tablet. The photos were shot on 35mm color-slide film using a Contax G2 camera (except for a few digital shots; you can write to me to find out more about those). No animals were harmed in the making of this book.

..and love always to T, A, and U.